UPLIFTING PIANO SOLOS

10 INSPIRING ARRANGEMENTS by GLENDA AUSTIN

T0039694

ISBN 978-1-70519-020-3

WILLIS MUSIC

Exclusively Distributed By

HAL•LEONARD®

Visit Hal Leonard Online at
www.halleonard.com

World headquarters, contact:
Hal Leonard
7777 West Bluemound Road
Milwaukee, WI 53213
Email: info@halleonard.com

In Europe, contact:
Hal Leonard Europe Limited
1 Red Place
London, W1K 6PL
Email: info@halleonardeurope.com

In Australia, contact:
Hal Leonard Australia Pty. Ltd.
4 Lentara Court
Cheltenham, Victoria, 3192 Australia
Email: info@halleonard.com.au

From the Arranger

This collection, *Uplifting Piano Solo*s, came together quickly, from conception to selection, to arranging and in print form.

Some thoughts along the way: I usually don't work this quickly (the arrangements needed to be written in one week). I was nervous. I was hesitant. And I was even a bit doubtful I could do what I promised. But, I was surprised at how quickly and easily it materialized. Ultimately, I love each song and each arrangement.

The collection is eclectic. It includes popular songs, folk melodies, and even a holiday tune. Some are intentionally unique to the style of the song as you might know it.

In giving suggestions of how to play, instead of being excessively wordy with detailed instructions, remember "less is more." I would like you to think of your own style and do what makes it come alive! That might include slowing, speeding, adding fermatas, slight pauses between phrases or sections—you get the idea.

More than anything, I want these solos to live up to the title and to uplift and inspire YOU to make your own music!

Happy playing!

Glenda Austin

April Showers

Words by B.G. DeSylva
Music by Louis Silvers
Arranged by Glenda Austin

Are You Lonesome Tonight?

Words and Music by Roy Turk
and Lou Handman
Arranged by Glenda Austin

Like a waltz, not too fast

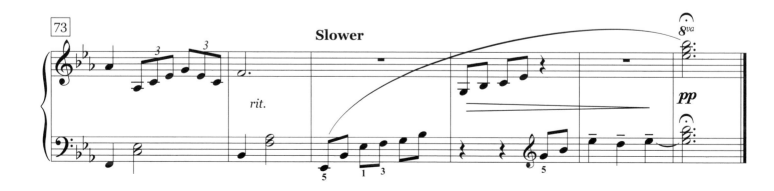

Danny Boy

Traditional Irish Folk Melody
Arranged by Glenda Austin

With rubato and flexibility

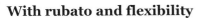

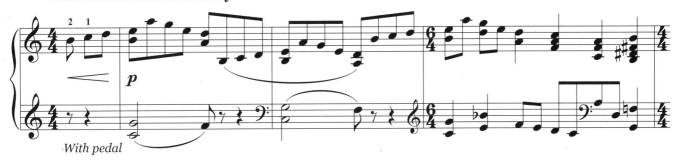

I Love a Piano

Words and Music by Irving Berlin
Arranged by Glenda Austin

It Had To Be You

Words by Gus Kahn
Music by Isham Jones
Arranged by Glenda Austin

Ode to Scotland
(Skye Boat Song and Loch Lomond)

Traditional
Arranged by Glenda Austin

Gently, with a lilt

The Missouri Waltz

Words by James Royce Shannon
Music by Frederick Knight Logan
Arranged by Glenda Austin

Scarborough Fair

Traditional English
Arranged by Glenda Austin

Not too fast

p *from a distance*

With pedal

Shenandoah

American Folksong
Arranged by Glenda Austin

Dreamily, with great liberty

With pedal

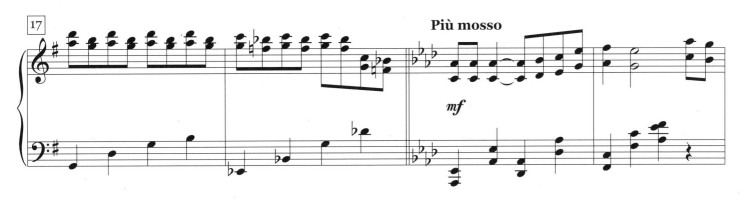

Ukrainian Bell Carol Fantasy

Traditional
Music by Mykola Leontovych
Arranged by Glenda Austin

With clear articulation and expression

MORE SOLOS BY GLENDA AUSTIN

00141980 Seven Minor Moods

00396981 Seasons

00171667 Holiday Encores

00324187 Three Jazz Suites

Glenda Austin was born and raised in Joplin, Missouri.

Recently retired from a lifetime of general music teaching, Glenda continues to be a pianist for various chamber and concert choirs at Missouri Southern State University. Along with composing and arranging, she regularly hosts Facebook Lives from her living room piano. She also has an active YouTube channel that showcases her diverse piano styles.

Glenda received her music degrees from the University of Missouri at Columbia. She is married to David, her hometown high school sweetheart, and they enjoy spending time with their family.